This is a Grandreams Book
This edition published in 2004

Grandreams Books Ltd, 4 North Parade, Bath BA1 1LF, UK

Designed and packaged by **Q2A Design Studio**
Printed in China

Step into the world of . . .

Pirates
and
Robbers

Contents

Ahoy There, Me Hearties!

Pirates, highwaymen and smugglers have always been subjects of great fascination. Stories of cops and robbers, smugglers' goods and hold-ups on highways never fail to excite us! But perhaps the most appealing of all were the pirates.

Portrait of a Pirate

Pirates — a word that conjures up visions of evil men, buried treasure, eye patches and pirate hats! Such portraits are largely the result of the fictional writer's imagination. But how close to reality is our idea of pirates? Were they all cruel killers who tortured prisoners? What kind of lives did they lead? Let's find out!

Scary eye patches and hats: symbols that come to mind when we think of pirates

Thieves at Sea

Pirates were robbers who sailed the seas and looted other ships for riches. They existed throughout history — as privateers, buccaneers, corsairs and marooners. They were all pirates, but differed from each other in some way. Though pirates have been raiding the seas for a long time, they flourished from the late 1600s to the 1720s — the Golden Age of Piracy.

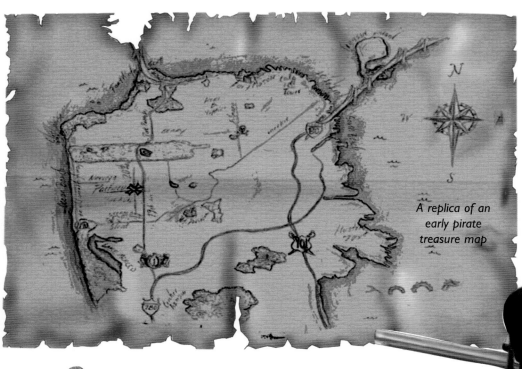

A replica of an early pirate treasure map

Did pirates really have treasure maps?

Treasure maps, with a big 'X' to mark the spot of buried treasure, are among the most fascinating part of pirate lore. Many believe that such maps never existed – except in story books and movies! However, a few pirates were thought to have marked out their hidden treasure.

Which group of pirates was named after barbecued meat?

Buccaneers lived on the islands of Hispaniola and Tortuga and hunted cattle and wild pigs for meat. Their method of barbecuing this meat on open fires and grills was called 'boucan' in French. When they were later paid by governors of the Caribbean islands to attack Spanish merchant vessels and harbours, they came to be known as buccaneers, from the word 'boucan!'

What does the word 'pirate' mean?

'Pirate' means someone who raids at sea. It is thought that the word *peirato* was first used around 140 B.C. by Polybius, a Roman historian. However, it is widely believed that the Greek historian Plutarch gave the first real definition of piracy. He wrote that pirates were those who attacked ships and maritime cities without legal authority.

Buccaneers became famous for their wild behaviour and acts of cruelty

One of the best dressed pirates was Black Bart, who wore waistcoats, breeches and a huge red feather in his hat!

How were privateers different from pirates?

Privateers also attacked other ships and stole valuables from them. However, they were different from pirates, because they were given a special license from their government to raid and capture pirate ships. This license was known as a Letter of Marque. Many privateers also became pirates once they saw how much money pirates had!

What kind of clothes did pirates wear?

Pirates often dressed in bright clothes that did not necessarily match! Of course, most pirates usually wore old and tattered clothes, but they changed if they managed to steal better outfits. The leader sometimes wore clothes made from costly silks that he looted from merchant ships.

Were the Vikings also pirates?

The Vikings of Scandinavia were fierce warriors who travelled to different parts of the world over 1000 years ago. Although they raided many ships for treasure, all Vikings were not pirates. Most were sailors in search of land to settle on.

Were there pirates in all parts of the world?

Pirates have been looting ships for years, in many different parts of the world. Pirates were active in the Mediterranean, Asia, Africa, Europe and the Americas.

FACT BOX

■ Nassau in the Bahamas was the heart and capital of the Golden Age of Piracy.

■ Pirates could become rich overnight, plundering gold and costly goods from merchant vessels. They would carry their wealth around in little pouches and waste no time in spending it!

Pirates were not the greatest of money-savers, spending most of what they looted in quick time!

■ Barbary corsairs were Islamic pirates who fought Christian corsairs along the Mediterranean Sea. They either got their name from their European enemies, who called them 'barbaric', or else from the Barbary Coast of North Africa, where they came from.

Ahoy There, Me Hearties!

What was the Jolly Roger?

The Jolly Roger flag is probably the most well known symbol of the pirate world. The flag, with a white skull and pair of crossbones on a black background, was used by many pirates of the 1700s. The Jolly Roger was meant to arouse fear in the enemy.

Pirates often referred to the Jolly Roger as Captain Death!

Why did some people choose to become pirates?

People became pirates for many reasons. Some turned to piracy when their ships were captured by pirates. Others joined pirate crews after serving as privateers. The lack of jobs after wars also forced many jobless sailors to turn to piracy.

Why did piracy start to fade away in the late 1800s?

Pirate activity came to a gradual end due to a variety of reasons. Better ocean surveillance by naval vessels made it difficult for pirates to attack. The widespread acceptance of piracy as a major crime also helped to reduce such incidents.

Is it true that pirates liked to drink a lot of alcohol?

Pirates were very fond of drinking rum and kept plenty stored in huge wooden barrels!

Who were corsairs?

Corsairs were seamen or privateers from France who sailed mostly on the Mediterranean Sea. Some corsairs, like the Barbary Corsairs of North Africa, were supported by their government to attack enemy ships.

The association between pirates and rum is so strong that a common nickname for rum is 'the pirate's drink'

Long, Long Ago...

Thousands of years ago, man began to sail to different lands for trade. As more and more people took to the oceans, tales of the pirate world began to unfold.

Proof of Pirates

The might of early sea raiders is evident from ancient myths and legends. One such myth tells us about Dionysus, the Greek God of Wine. Captured by pirates, Dionysus changed into a lion to scare his kidnappers, who jumped into the sea in fright. To punish them further, he turned the pirates into dolphins! This tale lives through ancient documents, mosaics and ceramic paintings.

An ancient Greek wine cup painted with the myth of Dionysus

And Off They Sailed...

As bigger and better ships were built, pirates from all around the world started a new legacy of crime and terror. Pirates of the Mediterranean and Aegean Seas established their own pirate empires. Vikings voyaged across the Atlantic and invaded many coastal cities of Europe. Japanese and Chinese sea robbers, too, spread fear across Asia. Soon, piracy became a threat for merchant ships everywhere! Pirates, with their savage ways, were certainly here to stay!

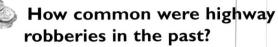

A medieval robber awaits his victim!

How common were highway robberies in the past?

Highway robberies, or robberies on the road, were quite widespread in the 1600s. Travellers often carried their money with them, because banks were not too common. Road signs and maps, too, were few in number. There were many jobless people who were desperate for money and they waited on lonely, deserted roads for travellers who they could rob at gun-point.

Did ancient pirates use stone catapults to fire at enemy ships?

Ancient pirates used a variety of weapons for battles at sea and on land. It is believed that the stone catapult was one such weapon used by ancient Greek and Roman pirates. In 2003, archaeologists discovered stone catapults at the ancient island-city of Antikythera in Greece.

Who were the Phoenicians?

Phoenicians were some of the earliest known pirates. Although they were legal traders in the Mediterranean, they occasionally looted merchant ships and towns along the coast.

Who was Polycrates?

Polycrates was a Greek dictator who forcefully took over the ancient city of Samos. He owned a fleet of 100 ships, which he used for practising piracy.

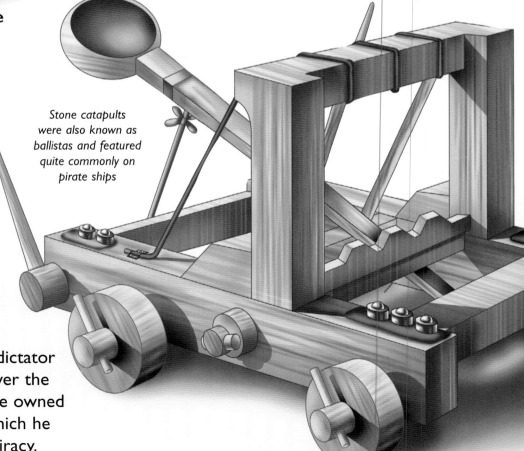

Stone catapults were also known as ballistas and featured quite commonly on pirate ships

Why did people fear the Barbary corsairs?

The Barbary corsairs were amongst the most feared group of pirates. They set up the Barbary States, their own empire that was headed by a government. They had pirate kings called raises and took their victims as slaves. Barbary corsairs were so fierce that they sometimes kidnapped children and demanded a price for them.

Another legend says that the name Barbary corsair originated from the Barbarossa brothers – two Greek-born brothers who became the most famous Barbary corsairs

How old is the practice of piracy?

There is no clear date to mark the beginning of piracy. However, it is known that pirates existed in ancient civilisations. One of the first documents to mention pirates dates back to 1350 B.C. It was a report carved into a clay tablet describing shipping attacks in North Africa.

Why did ancient Greek pirates like the Aegean Sea?

Much of the ancient Greek civilisation developed around the Aegean Sea. Greek pirates used this to their advantage. They hid on the Aegean islands and took merchant ships by surprise.

FACT BOX

- In the past, some people believed that pirates had certain good qualities. Pirates who were brave and daring and were good leaders were therefore often treated with respect and honour!

- King Shapur of Persia (309-379 A.D.) was known for waging battles against pirates in the Persian Gulf. Legend has it that he pierced the shoulders of the pirates and roped them all together! For this, he earned the nickname, Zulaklaf, which means Lord of the Shoulders!

The custom of painting eyes on ancient sailing vessels may have originated in ancient Egypt

- Ancient Greek and Roman pirates often painted eyes on their ships for good luck! They believed that the eyes of their gods and goddesses would protect them from dangers ahead.

Chinese pirate junks could accommodate up to 15 guns

What kind of sailing vessel did ancient Chinese pirates use?

Chinese pirates sailed in junks to allow for easy and fast movement. Junks were also good for tricking enemy ships. Most Chinese merchants also sailed in junks, so it was difficult for them to sight a pirate junk until it was much too late!

Were there any laws against piracy in ancient times?

A law against piracy did exist in ancient Rome! It was recorded in a document of rules for dealing with piracy, dating back to 100 B.C.

How organised were pirates in ancient China?

The pirates of ancient China were known to be very organised. They kept records and drew up contracts for everything. They even kept records of the payments they received from their victims!

Who were the corsairs of Malta?

The corsairs of Malta fought against the Barbary corsairs. They helped the Knights of Malta to wage wars against the Islamic invaders, but, gradually, they too became interested in the riches of piracy!

What kind of ships did ancient Greek and Roman pirates use?

Greek and Roman pirates liked to use galleys like triremes to ram holes into enemy ships. Galleys were lightweight and had shallow bottoms, which made them fast and easy to move.

The trireme represented the sea power of the pirates of ancient Greece

Highwaymen and Smugglers

Road robbers, outlaws, brigands and smugglers have intrigued one and all as much as pirates. Their adventures, escapades and signature styles of robbing people earned them an image that was almost heroic!

Robbers and Raiders

There is no telling when theft and robbery began. Ever since man has existed, raiders and robbers have flourished. There were highway robbers, smugglers, bandits and outlaws – to name a few. Rapparees, too, were well-known. They were soldiers who became raiders in 17th-century Ireland. They were named so for their dagger-like weapons called 'raparies.' From Dick Turpin to the Hawkhurst Gang, many of these land robbers created a place for themselves in the history of crime.

Smuggling

Smuggling began with thieves practising illegal trade on a small scale. Gradually, smugglers started operating in groups and gangs, transporting costly goods without paying taxes for them.

Tobacco leaves and cocoa beans for making chocolate were amongst the most common goods smuggled across Europe

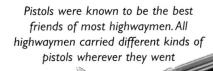

Pistols were known to be the best friends of most highwaymen. All highwaymen carried different kinds of pistols wherever they went

Was anything done to make robbing more difficult for highwaymen?

In the early 1800s, highwaymen became more cautious. Police forces became more organised and law enforcement improved. Roads were also developed and were less isolated than they used to be. Such factors led to the gradual disappearance of the traditional highwayman.

Did highwaymen carry any weapons?

Highwaymen usually carried pistols to threaten people to get off their stagecoaches and hand over their riches.

What is smuggling?

Smuggling is the name given to any unlawful transportation of goods from one country to another. It is unlawful because smuggled goods are not brought in with government permission. This allows smugglers to avoid paying taxes on the goods. These are then sold illegally, at cheaper prices.

Did smugglers ever get caught?

Smugglers often got caught while getting away with their own share of expensive weapons, treasure and barrels of rum! In many countries, punishments for smugglers were harsh. However, smugglers who got caught were very sometimes let off easily!

Caught in the act: two smugglers on the run are arrested by the police

Rope was an important part of a highwayman's kit

Why did some highwaymen carry ropes with them?

Most highwaymen were known to have a special method or style of robbing travellers. Some of them would first force their victims to hand over goods or money and then tie them with rope to a tree or any other object on the road!

What things were commonly smuggled in the past?

Smuggling has been practiced for thousands of years. In the past, expensive goods such as wine, silk and tea were smuggled into countries by boats at night. Goods were also smuggled in by land, either on horseback or by other means.

During which period of history were highway robberies very common?

Highway robberies were most common during the 16th-18th centuries. They especially flourished in 17th and 18th-century England.

How did highwaymen disguise themselves?

Highwaymen often wore masks over the upper part of their faces to make sure their victims would not be able to recognise them later.

Who were highwaymen?

Highwaymen were criminals who stopped travellers on public roads and highways. They were usually on horseback.

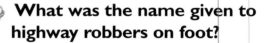

Eye masks made it easy for highwaymen to keep their identities a secret

What was the name given to highway robbers on foot?

Road robbers who did not have horses were known as footpads. Footpads committed the same kind of crimes as highwaymen, but on foot.

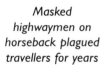

Masked highwaymen on horseback plagued travellers for years

Why was it so easy for highwaymen to attack travellers?

More often than not, travelling routes were set along lonely roads in the countryside. Highwaymen found it easy to hide along these routes and attack travellers by surprise, especially as there was hardly anyone around to help.

Why were highwaymen more successful than footpads?

Footpads found it difficult to chase carriages and coaches that tried to escape. Highwaymen were far more successful, because they could keep up with their victims on horseback.

Scourges of the Seven Seas

Calico Jack, Samuel Bellamy, Black Bart, Dick Turpin — they were amongst the kings of the thieving world. Certain robbers became time-honoured criminals with their terrifying ways!

The Pirate of All Pirates

He mixed gunpowder in his rum and braided his long beard with ribbons. Britain's Edward Teach, better known as Blackbeard, is without doubt the most famous pirate of all time. Here was a rogue who supposedly sliced off a passenger's finger when refused the diamond ring on it! From crew members to enemies, he scared everyone. Stealing the ship, *Queen Anne's Revenge*, he sailed the Caribbean Sea and the Atlantic Ocean during 1716-1718.

In 1718, Blackbeard hosted a party at his hideout in Ocracoke Island. Virginia's governor, Alexander Spotswood heard of this and planned to capture Blackbeard. Naval seamen, headed by Robert Maynard, took the unprepared pirates by surprise. Maynard eventually killed Blackbeard, hanging the feared pirate's head from his ship to prove that he was finally dead!

Blackbeard's end was one of the goriest events in the history of piracy

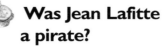

Was Jean Lafitte a pirate?

Jean Lafitte was a famous American privateer-turned-pirate and smuggler. He was best known for smuggling slaves.

Before becoming a privateer, Jean Lafitte ran a blacksmith shop with his brother, which was said to be used for smuggling slaves

Which privateers went on to become famous pirates?

Amongst the famous privateers who became pirates were Sir Henry Morgan, Blackbeard and Captain William Kidd.

Who is considered to be one of the most cruel pirates to have ever lived?

Edward Low, a Caribbean pirate, was known for his cruel ways. It is believed that he cut off people's lips or ears when he wanted to punish them!

Why was Major Stede Bonnet considered to the most unlikely pirate?

Major Stede Bonnet, a famous English pirate, was perhaps the most unlikely pirate of all time. He was educated, came from a well-to-do family and made a good living with his own sugar plantations. Bonnet was often called the 'gentleman pirate,' and was known to be the only pirate to buy ships, instead of stealing them!

Which famous privateer fought against the Spanish Armada?

Sir Francis Drake led England to victory against the fleet of ships known as the Spanish Armada. The Spaniards had named it the 'Invincible Armada', believing it to be un-defeatable. However, Sir Francis Drake became a national hero when he defeated it in 1588.

Captain William Kidd's signature was known for its big, sweeping W and a giant swirling K

Which famous legend did Captain Kidd start?

Captain Kidd, one of the most famous pirates of all time, started the timeless legend of buried pirate treasure. He captured the *Quedah Merchant*, a vessel that was said to have goods worth more than $100,000! He was later arrested and tried in court, where he was found guilty and hanged.

Which famous smuggling gang was named after their home village?

The Hawkhurst Gang (1735 A.D. –1749 A.D.) was one of the most famous gangs of smugglers to have existed. They were named after the English village they lived in.

The Spanish Armada, a fleet of one hundred and fifty ships, sailed to invade England in 1588

FACT BOX

- Alvilda was one of the first woman pirate captains. She formed an all-woman pirate crew and sailed to sea in order to escape getting married to a Danish Prince.

- Blackbeard was said to own a pet parrot who scoffed at prisoners while they were tortured!

The parrot became a major symbol of the pirate world thanks to Long John Silver, the fictional character from Treasure Island

- One of the first-ever highwaymen was not a man, but a woman! Mary Frith, who came from London, came to be known as Moll Cutpurse!

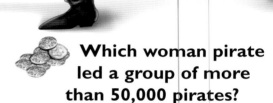

Who was the first woman pirate to sail in the Caribbean?

Around the 1720s, Ann Bonny became the first woman pirate to sail in the Caribbean. Bonny started her life as a pirate when she boarded a pirate ship dressed as a man. She went on to become one of the toughest and hardiest pirates around.

Ann Bonny was said to be an expert at firing pistols and stabbing rapiers. She was as dangerous as her male crew members

Who was the Gallant Highwayman?

Claude Duval was called the 'Gallant Highwayman' due to his charming ways. His most written-about exploit was his hold-up of a nobleman and his lady. The lady played a flageolet (a kind of flute) so as to appear unafraid. Duval also took out a flageolet and began to play. He told the nobleman he wanted to dance with the lady. After they had danced for a while, Duval told her that the nobleman hadn't paid him for the music. Duval then took 400 pounds from the nobleman and left!

Duval's gravestone was marked with the following words – "Here lies Duval, Reader if male thou art, Look to thy purse: if female to thy heart"!

Which woman pirate led a group of more than 50,000 pirates?

Cheng I Sao of China was one of the most famous woman pirates. She took charge of more than 50,000 pirates in the early 1800s!

Which place in the Bahamas is named after Henry Morgan?

The highest point of Andros Island in the Bahamas was named Morgan's Bluff after Sir Henry Morgan. He is once said to have hung a lantern here to mislead a merchant vessel towards some rocks. When the ship was wrecked, he stole all its goods!

Which other famous woman pirate became good friends with Ann Bonny?

Mary Read and Ann Bonny met on pirate 'Calico' Jack Rackham's ship. Bonny fell in love with Mary Read by mistake, who was dressed as a man! Later, Read revealed her true identity to Bonny and the two became good friends.

All Aboard!

We usually associate the lives of pirates with adventure and excitement. But this was not always the case!

Boredom and Danger

Sailing for days on end, pirates often got bored on their voyages. With little to do, they whiled away their time by eating, playing games or fighting among themselves! Excitement came occasionally, when an enemy vessel was spotted. During battle, their seemingly boring lives took a sudden turn from dullness to extreme danger!

The Swift Ol' Schooner!

Any ship taken over by pirates became a pirate ship. However, pirates did have preferences for certain vessels. Their favourite was the schooner. With its small and narrow hull (frame), it could hide in tiny inlets and move fast in both shallow and deep waters. It was also sturdy, fit to carry a crew of over 70 and even more weapons and goods. No wonder the schooner was the ultimate dreamboat for most pirates!

Schooners were especially popular with North American and Caribbean pirates

How did pirates find their way at sea?

Pirates used a variety of navigation instruments to find their way around at sea. These included the magnetic compass, the backstaff, sundials, lodestones, telescopes and waggoners. Waggoners were books of maps and charts.

Pirates boarded the enemy ship with grappling hooks, axes, ropes and pulleys

What did pirates use to determine the position of stars?

Pirates used the astrolabe to measure the height of the sun and stars. This helped them to understand the position of their ships. During the age of pirates, this ancient instrument was called the 'astrolaby'.

Without the astrolabe, pirates would have had a difficult time figuring out where their ship was going!

How did most pirates attack ships at mid-sea?

Every pirate crew had their own way of attacking vessels. However, most crews liked to take their enemy by surprise, boarding the ship quickly by jamming its rudder, so that it could not move. Pirates also used weapons if their victims put up a fight.

Essentially trading ships, caravels could carry over 1000 kg (100 tons) of cargo! This made them useful for pirates, who travelled in large numbers and with many heavy weapons

What kind of ships did pirates sail in?

Pirates sailed in all kinds of vessels. Some of the most popular included brigantines, sloops, schooners, junks, galleys and caravels. Caravels were lightweight ships that were useful for pirates, as they could sail fast, even against strong winds. They could also carry a lot of goods.

Did pirates follow any rules at sea?

Most pirates followed a certain code of conduct while at sea. The rules included putting out all the lights by eight o'clock at night and keeping their weapons clean and ready for use at all times.

Why did pirates avoid attacking slave ships?

Slave ships were usually quite big, with a lot of people on board. Some pirate crews preferred to avoid attacking such ships, as this meant wastage of weapons and gunfire.

What rights did pirate crew members have?

Each pirate was allowed to vote on which ships to attack or where to go. Crew members also had the right to elect a new leader, if they felt that the existing captain was not good enough.

What food and drink did pirates carry on board?

Pirates kept a stock of long-lasting food and drink, because they often travelled for long periods at a stretch. They kept bottles of beer and barrels of rum, as the water they drank became too salty after a while. Limes were an important source of vitamin C for warding off scurvy. Some pirates also took hens with them for eggs and meat.

From which other animal did pirates get meat?

The turtles of the Caribbean Sea were a common source of meat for pirates while sailing. They were easy to catch, because they moved slowly. They were said to taste quite good too!

Did the pirate captain have his own cabin?

Most pirates slept in cramped quarters below the deck. The captain had his own cabin in the quarterdeck, where the helm (steering wheel) of the ship was. The captain's cabin was usually small but well equipped, with a desk, maps, a globe and navigational tools. Everyone was allowed to use the captain's cabin.

Compasses like this one were kept in special boxes aboard pirate decks. The boxes were called binnacles

Was the captain of a pirate ship very powerful?

The captain of a pirate ship was the person who owned and sailed the ship. The head of the pirate crew was only the leader of his group during battles and not the ship. He was elected by his crew members. He made decisions on boarding and attacking enemy ships or raiding lands. The captain, who steered the vessel, received the same amount of booty as the leader.

How did pirates work on board?

Work aboard pirate ships was equally divided among crew members. This way, daily jobs were completed more easily and fairly.

The captain's cabin also contained a bed and a footlocker for storing clothes in

Land Ho!

Pirates were not only fearless sea raiders. They were just as happy to plunder the towns and colonies they visited!

Way Back Then...

Since the early ages, pirates, privateers and buccaneers were skilled at raiding towns and villages. They often forced people out of their homes, threatening to kill women and children and holding people hostage inside churches. The Barbary corsairs and buccaneers like Henry Morgan were especially feared for their attacks. In the 1800s, Chinese pirates were said to write letters of threat to people in coastal towns for money. The poor villagers had to pay up or else be enslaved by pirates.

Moving About

On land, pirates either moved on foot or used common modes of land transport. They also rode on horseback for a quick getaway after attacks. Horse-drawn wagons and caravans were occasionally used. These were usually plundered from villagers or travellers.

The wagon: a common mode of transport in the early days

Why did pirates stop on land from time to time?

After travelling continuously for months, pirates not only had to rest, but also had to stock up on food when their supplies were over. Most importantly, they had to bring their ships to shore for careening, or cleaning the weeds, worms and barnacles from the bottom of the vessel. When free, they liked to spend the money they had stolen from merchant vessels.

A pirate lazes on the beach with a drink!

What did pirates eat on deserted islands?

When pirates pulled ashore on a deserted island, they looked out for animals like monkeys, birds and goats for meat. They chased these animals with clubs and sometimes even caught them with bare hands!

Where on land did pirates often go to celebrate their victories?

Pirates loved to visit taverns, or pubs, that stayed open till late at night. They would sit there for hours, drinking. They were so fond of alcohol that they sometimes spent much of what they had plundered on barrels of rum!

Which active game did pirates sometimes play on land?

Pirates often had sword fights or duels on land. It was a popular form of entertainment for them. Two people would have a sword-fighting competition, while the other crew members watched. Duels were also held to settle important issues.

Members of a pirate crew often fought duels to decide who would be captain or how the booty would be divided

A pirate cleans his rifle at shore

FACT BOX

- Pirates on land used a method called caulking while repairing their ships. In caulking, the gaps between the ship's planks were fixed to make the vessel watertight.

- Pirates were served beer, wine, rum and other alcoholic drinks in pewter or leather tankards called Black Jacks. The keepers at taverns knew that serving drinks to drunk pirates in glass mugs would cost them dearly!

Did pirates only clean their ships when they pulled up on shore?

While on land, pirates also spent a lot of time cleaning their weapons. It was not always possible to do so properly on board a ship and pirates looked forward to going ashore and giving their rifles a thorough clean!

Black Jacks were watertight and sturdy, as they were made of leather and coated with tar

Why did some people welcome pirates on their land?

Some people did not mind pirates visiting them. This was because pirates often sold their stolen goods to local people at cheaper prices!

Is it true that pirates usually preferred to land on deserted islands?

Most pirates liked to pull ashore on isolated islands, because they were not always welcome in places where there were a lot of people. Staying on a deserted beach also suited them, for it served as a good hideout.

- When pirates went ashore, many were not satisfied with a break. They often took to the shores in order to attack and plunder colonies or towns.

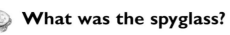

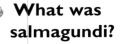

What was the spyglass?

Spyglass was the name that pirates gave to their telescope.

Pirates called their telescopes by the nickname, 'bring 'em near'!

What was salmagundi?

Salmagundi was a favourite meal of the pirates. It was a salad that consisted of chopped meat, eggs, anchovies and onions. Often served on lettuce leaves, salmagundi was also occasionally flavoured with vinegar and oil.

Where did pirates sleep on land?

Pirates usually set up tents on the shore to sleep in. Some pirates made their tents with old ship sails.

How else did pirates spend their money?

Pirates also liked to spend their money on pretty women they met on land!

Always on the lookout!

Did pirates use spyglasses on land?

Even when pirates took a break ashore, they would often climb on treetops and look through spyglasses. They did so to keep a look out for other pirate ships and merchant vessels.

Blow 'Em Down!

The cracking shot of a rifle, the thundering boom of cannons and the brilliant flash of clashing swords! This is just a taste of what life must have been like for battling pirates at sea.

Fighting with Fear!

Hundreds of frenzied pirates boarded enemy ships with no fear whatsoever for anyone or anything. They paralysed their victims with fear even before boarding the ship, with danger signals, loud war cries, heavily-armed ships and cannon fire.

Pirates fired cannonballs only to destroy a ship's sails and rigging. The intention was to frighten the enemy, not to destroy the ship. Pirates did not like to sink any vessels, because they valued the ship as a treasure.

Loaded with their flintlock pistols, glistening axes and hand grenades made of bottles and gunpowder, pirates finally boarded the enemy ship and quickly emerged as victors more often than not!

More than 20 lead cannons could be mounted on a large pirate ship!

27

Which common pirate weapon was an early form of the rifle?

The musket, an early weapon commonly used by pirates, was a model for the present-day rifle. Pirates used muskets to fire from a distance, since they were less effective at close range.

The long musket rifle was usually fired from the shoulder at long distance targets

Pirates often used a combination of the cutlass and pistol. Known as a hunter's sword, this gave pirates the advantage of using two weapons at one go

Which group of pirates were said to have invented the cutlass?

The cutlass, a common seafaring weapon, is believed to have been invented by the buccaneers. It originated from the long knives that buccaneers used to butcher meat with. The cutlass was a short sword with a wide blade that was convenient for hand-to-hand battles on crowded ships.

Which pirate weapon gave rise to the word, 'bombardment'?

Many pirate ships had bombards on their ships. The bombard was an early form of the cannon and was used for firing heavy cannonballs made of stone. In fact, the word 'bombardment' originated from the bombard.

The bombard was loaded with stone shots instead of lead or iron ones

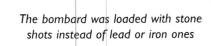

Why were pirate attacks successful most of the time?

Most pirate attacks were successful. This was because their ships carried many more people than enemy ships of the same size. Pirates won battles thanks to the sheer number of their crew members.

What did Blackbeard once demand as ransom for a group of captive children?

Blackbeard once took the passengers of a cargo ship hostage. There were children on this ship too. He locked them up inside a dark area and threatened to kill them if the local villagers did not meet his demands. He had asked for a chest of medicines!

Did pirates carry a lot of weapons aboard their ships?

Pirates carried a variety of weapons on board their ships. Though they weren't always used, it was important to stock up on them in case of surprise attacks.

What were stinkpots?

One of the most interesting pirate weapons was the stinkpot. Stinkpots were pots filled with chemicals, which let out a bad smell when set on fire! Pirates would fling these pots on to the decks of enemy ships to suffocate their victims with the stink!

FACT BOX

■ Most sailors stayed barefoot on wet and slippery decks. Pirates took advantage of this and threw crowsfeet on to the decks of enemy ships. These were sharp spikes that injured sailors who stepped on them!

■ Powderhorns were used by pirates for storing gunpowder. They were not usually taken into battle, as pirates loaded their weapons long before they attacked.

The powderhorn was vital to a pirate's armour, as wet gunpowder would make his gunfire completely useless

■ When pirates won a battle and took over an enemy ship, they carried out a ritual called 'strike colours.' This was the practice of pulling down the ship's flag to symbolise its surrender.

Blow 'Em Down!

Swivel guns or cannons were lined up along the railing of a pirate ship

 How did Blackbeard trick enemy ships?

After spotting his target, Blackbeard raised the enemy ship's national flag to appear friendly, hoisting his pirate flag only when it was too late!

 What were swivel guns?

Swivel guns were small weapons similar to cannons. They were so called because they were mounted on swivels (rotating axles) on the sides of a ship. Pirates could swing these guns and shoot at the deck of an enemy ship in one sweep!

 Was the blunderbuss a weapon?

The blunderbuss was a gun used by pirates for short-range firing. It had a funnel-shaped barrel that allowed the firing of several bullets, that took off in many different directions!

 What was the No Quarter?

Pirates flew a long red banner from their ship masts to let enemies know that they were going to attack. This signal was called the 'No Quarter.'

Cruel-hearted pirates were known to add tiny bits of metal or bone to the twisted cords of the cat o' nine tails!

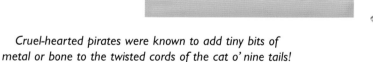

 Which pirate weapon was named after a common house pet?

Pirates used a weapon called the 'cat o' nine tails.' It was made up of nine frayed bits of rope, which were attached to a handle grip. It was used for beating prisoners and hostages on their bare backs!

Torture and Punishment

"*If one brother steals from another, his nose or ears are to be cut off*". Pirates were a mean bunch indeed! They not only punished disobedient pirates, but also prisoners and slaves. Sometimes, victims were tormented for fun!

Cruel Customs

Whipping, beating and bruising – pirates were known for their cruel ways. Buccaneers, too, were said to hurt their prisoners with matchsticks and knives.

Dance of Death

When pirates were caught, they were usually hanged. Fearless pirates called it 'dancing the hempen jig.' They were referring to the hanging as a kind of death dance, on a rope made of hemp!

Sentenced pirates were taken to an execution dock where the hanging gallows awaited them. This was a wooden frame with a noose tied to it. Before being hanged, pirates were allowed to address the public, who were always glad to watch executions! While some pirates appeared to be sorry, others shamelessly told jokes!

Gallows like this one were specially made before each execution

Torture and Punishment

WANTED

Henery Morgan

How did law officials capture pirates?

Law officials had to look very hard for pirates and robbers, who had hideouts that were very difficult to find. Very often, posters with a pirate's portrait were pasted all over villages and towns, offering a reward for information about the criminal's whereabouts.

Putting up 'wanted' posters was a popular method for tracing the most wanted pirates and robbers

Walking the plank: this form of torture was used more by pirates in China than those of North America and the Caribbean

What were pirate charters?

Most pirates followed a certain set of rules relating to their conduct. These sets of rules were known as charters.

Which form of punishment was rarely used by pirates?

One of the most famous pirate legends is walking the plank. Pirates were thought to tie the hands of their victims and make them walk off a plank of wood, into the sea! Walking the plank has featured as a common part of pirate life in books and films. However, this was seldom done in reality.

What was the gibbet cage?

The gibbet cage was a wooden or iron frame in which the dead bodies of the most infamous pirates were locked. The body was first covered with tar and then suspended at a public place from the gibbet.

Were pirates ever punished for torturing their victims?

Piracy was a major crime during the Golden Age of Piracy. Any pirate or robber who was caught by a legal officer or the government of a nation was severely punished. The more dangerous a pirate was reputed to be, the worse was his treatment. At some maritime prisons in England, their bodies were hung above water, and removed only after three tides had washed over them!

What did pirates sign before they officially became crew members?

All pirates had to sign an agreement before they became members of a crew. The agreement contained articles, which held information on how much the pirate would be paid, what he was allowed and forbidden to do as well as the punishments for breaking rules.

Who judged whether a pirate was guilty?

All accused pirates underwent a proper trial to decide if they deserved punishment. The members of the pirate crew served as the panel of judges.

Gibbet cages were tailor-made to fit the corpses, so that the skeleton stayed in place after the flesh had decayed

FACT BOX

■ Most pirates did not treat their slaves and prisoners well. They were often tied up in gang chains and ankle fetters. Gang chains were used to chain slaves attempting to revolt, while ankle fetters on the feet kept them from escaping.

■ Scotsman Alexander Selkirk was perhaps the only privateer to request that he be marooned! By the time he changed his mind, his ship had sailed off, leaving him on a deserted island. This story inspired Daniel Defoe's *Robinson Crusoe*.

■ The early handcuffs for arresting robbers were similar to the ones used nowadays, except that they were more likely to be made of iron, rather than steel.

A set of early handcuffs

Were pirates and robbers always locked in prison cells when arrested?

In the early days of crime, when prison cells were not so common, robbers were arrested and locked up in pillories. These were wooden frames with holes for the prisoner's head and arms. He would be locked in the pillory at a public place, while people threw stones at him and ridiculed him.

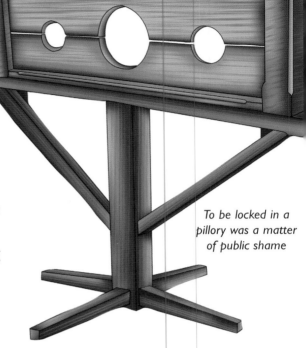

To be locked in a pillory was a matter of public shame

 What punishments were given to pirates who broke rules?

The kind of punishment a pirate received depended on the rule he broke. If a pirate stole from a fellow crew member, he was either killed or marooned after having his ears and nose slashed. Sometimes, they were tied to the ship's mast and whipped with the cat o' nine tails. For disobeying minor rules, pirates were either fined or not given their share of treasure.

Pirates and robbers were sometimes locked in stocks instead of pillories

What was the worst punishment for a pirate who broke rules?

If pirates broke certain rules of the articles, they were marooned. This involved being left alone on a deserted island with very little to eat and drink and only one pistol for protection. Most marooned pirates gradually died of hunger and thirst.

Which prison tool was similar to the pillory?

The stock was just like the pillory, except that a criminal's feet could also be locked in it.

Were pirates allowed to bring women with them to sea?

The pirate code of conduct did not allow any women on board a pirate ship! Only women who were pirates were allowed to travel with a pirate crew.

Bring in the Booty!

Pirates might have loved their dangerous way of life, full of battles, voyages and escapades. But there was only one driving force behind every pirate – treasure!

Secrets Untold!

The legend of pirate treasure is a timeless one, filled with visions of gold coins, jewels and overflowing treasure chests! Captain Cook, Benito Bonito, 'Calico' Jack, Captain Kidd, Blackbeard, Jean Lafitte – they were all thought to have buried their booty at some point in time. And the deserted island, with its swaying palm trees and golden beds of sand, was the favourite hiding ground.

Though the treasures of most pirates remain unproven stories, tales of pirate treasure are many. The most famous of them all was that of Captain Kidd's. Were it not for the recovery of his buried booty, we would never have known that pirates did, indeed, bury treasure. Then there was Jean Lafitte, who is said to have had so many riches that he buried them separately in many different places!

Some merchant ships were so full of riches that pirates could become rich overnight

Bring in the Booty!

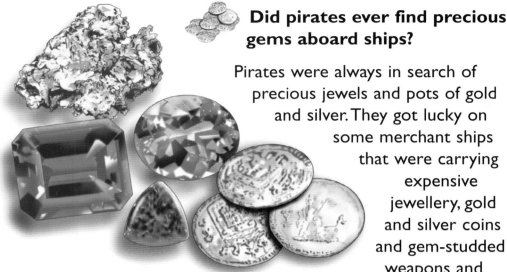

Did pirates ever find precious gems aboard ships?

Pirates were always in search of precious jewels and pots of gold and silver. They got lucky on some merchant ships that were carrying expensive jewellery, gold and silver coins and gem-studded weapons and artefacts.

Gold and precious stones were the most difficult treasures to divide fairly amongst the crew!

What kind of treasures did pirates usually find on merchant ships?

The 'treasures' that pirates plundered included grain, barrels of rum and wine, fine silks, sugar, spices, medicines, fish, wood, iron, slaves and weapons.

What was Captain William Kidd said to do each time he buried treasure?

Legend has it that whenever Captain Kidd buried treasure, he killed one of his crew members and threw him in with the treasure before covering up the pit! He did this because he believed that the dead pirate's spirit would protect the riches from treasure hunters!

The fabled buried treasure of Captain William Kidd

By the end of the 17th century, the diving bell had become popular for exploring shipwrecks and sunken treasures

What do divers use to look for treasure underwater?

Archaeologists and divers often use the diving bell to look for shipwrecks and treasures underwater. The diving bell is a mechanism used to move between the surface and lower depths of oceans and seas.

Did pirates steal clothes from their victims?

Clothes were among the most common goods plundered by pirates from attacked ships. They would then wear many of these clothes, mixing and matching strange colours together!

Why were pirates selective about the ships they attacked?

Pirates chose their target ships carefully. They selected only those ships that looked likely to have enough treasure on board.

What happened to pirate captains if they failed to steal enough riches?

Any captain who was considered to be ineffective in raiding ships for treasure was removed from his post by his own crew.

FACT BOX

- Pieces of eight were also called reales and doubloons were known as escudos. One side of the doubloon was inscribed with two columns symbolising the Pillars of Hercules. The pillars became a popular symbol of money and it is believed that the dollar sign originated from them!

- Although pirates wore most of the clothes they plundered, they never liked to wear slops, the striped top worn by sailors in Britain!

- The spot where Captain Kidd's treasure was buried was marked with a stone. The stone is inscribed with the year in which the treasure was discovered.

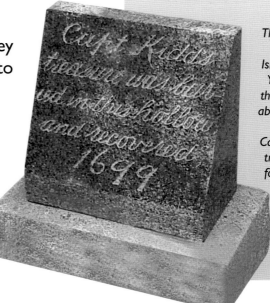

This stone, on Gardiner's Island in New York, marks the site where about £14,000 worth of Captain Kidd's treasure was found buried

Which treasures were used by pirates as money?

The most favourite treasure of pirates was Spanish coins. They stole silver coins, called pieces of eight, and cut them up for small change. Doubloons, or Spanish gold coins, were even more valuable. A single doubloon was worth nearly double the monthly salary of an ordinary sailor!

Gold and silver coins in the pirate world were known as specie

How did pirates bury their treasure?

Some pirates buried their stolen goods in secret hideouts. They sometimes placed this treasure in huge treasure chests, which they called coffers.

Were any treasures found aboard the only recovered pirate shipwreck?

In 1984, *Whydah*, the only known pirate shipwreck, was discovered. Among the treasures found on it were hoards of gold and silver.

How was pirate treasure distributed among the members of the crew?

Most crew members received an equal share of the booty. The captain and the ship's pilot, however, got more than the others. Another share was kept aside to cover the costs of maintaining the ship.

What happened if a crew failed to steal any treasures?

Nobody in the pirate crew was paid if there was no booty!

The pirates' charter of articles provided specific rules for the division of booty

Did You Know?

For years, the pirate has been a legendary figure. In books, films, plays and mythical tales, pirates have thrilled and chilled us through the ages!

The Legendary Pirate

From Long John Silver to Captain Hook, classic fiction like *Treasure Island* and *Peter Pan* created a popular image of the pirate. The evil, filthy and drunken sea robber with eye patches, wooden legs and hook hands took shape from imagination and settled forever in our minds. In fact, much of what we believe about pirates is drawn from this!

The character of Captain Hook in J.M. Barrie's Peter Pan was thought to have been partly inspired by Blackbeard

Fact and Fiction

Though many pirates were ruthless, not all were fearsome murderers. Our ideas of pirates are mostly a mix of myths and facts. Yes, pirates were believed to have pet parrots. But did you know they also kept black cats for good luck? Pirates did lose their limbs, but the hook hand and peg leg were the creations of writers and filmmakers. And so, the pirate lives on as a timeless symbol of adventure!

This medal was issued to honour the German pirate, Störtebeker. Executed in 1401, Störtebeker, was known as the Robin Hood of his region

 Which pirate left a crew he captured inside barrels of herring fish?

The famous German pirate, Klaus Störtebeker, once left his captives in herring barrels! Störtebeker was the leader of the Vital Brothers, a group of pirates who were active on the Baltic and North Seas.

How did the Jolly Roger get its name?

It is believed that the name Jolly Roger came from the French description for early privateer flags, *jolie rouge*, which means 'pretty red.' The Jolly Roger motif of skull and crossbones was first seen sometime in 1700, when a French pirate named Emanuel Wynne flew a black flag with the picture of a skull, crossed bones and hourglass on it.

Did all pirate ships fly the Jolly Roger?

No, all pirates did not fly the Jolly Roger. Each pirate captain had his own special flag. For example, 'Calico' Jack had one with a skull and crossed swords, instead of crossed bones. Other pirate captains had a combination of skulls, skeletons, swords and daggers on their flags.

Nearly every pirate had his or her own flag – with different motifs to symbolise death – such as hour glasses, swords, skull, bones and bleeding hearts

Did pirates smoke?

Pirates loved to smoke tobacco from long, clay pipes. However, they could only do so while on shore, for they were not allowed to smoke aboard their ship. Pirate ships were wooden, and smoking on board could lead to a fire.

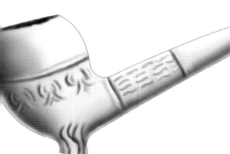

Pirates smoked tobacco from clay pipes like this one

What were pirates said to eat when food was finished and there was no land in sight?

It is believed that in desperate situations, pirate crews would eat their leather satchels! We know this from a recipe written by one of Sir Henry Morgan's crew members: "...*slice the leather into pieces then soak, beat and rub between stones to tenderize. Scrape off the hair, then roast or grill. Cut into smaller pieces and serve with lots of water...*"!

When was the Yellow Jack flag flown?

The Yellow Jack was a yellow flag that was flown to show that somebody on board was ill with yellow fever or some other disease. Many sailors flew this flag from their ships to trick pirates away!

What happened to pirates who became disabled?

When pirates became disabled in battle, they were paid money. The right arm was worth the most, at 600 pieces of eight. An eye or finger was worth 100. If a pirate lost both legs or both arms, they were compensated with 800 pieces of eight and a slave. Pirates were perhaps the first to have an insurance system!

FACT BOX

- Chinese pirate flags often had images of bats on them. The Chinese believed that the bat was a symbol of good fortune.

- The first man with tattoos to be displayed publicly was Prince Joely. Also known as Giolo, he was brought to England in 1691 by the famous buccaneer, William Dampier.

- Many pirate ships, especially those which sailed on the Spanish Main, were decorated with elaborate motifs and designs, carved intricately in gold.

Pirate ships were often beautifully decorated with animal figurines carved in gold

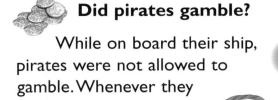

Did pirates gamble?

While on board their ship, pirates were not allowed to gamble. Whenever they went ashore, pirates gambled their money on card games.

Pirates played with cards such as these in their spare time

Who was Francis L'Ollonais?

Francis L'Ollonais was one of the craziest buccaneers to have lived. The Frenchman was known to first torture his prisoners and then cut them up!

What did pirates believe they had to do to improve their eyesight?

Some pirates thought that piercing their ears and wearing silver or gold earrings would improve their vision!

What was the highest deck on a pirate ship called?

The highest deck on a pirate ship was called the poop deck! It was usually situated above the pirate captain's cabin.

What were cannon shots?

Pirates had different types of shots to put through their cannons. The bar shot, which looked a little like a dumbbell, was used to destroy the sails of enemy ships. Even better than the bar shot was the chain shot. This was also used to destroy sails and other ship parts. With a chain attached to two cannon balls, the chain shot attacked with greater speed and force.

The bar shot, cannon ball and chain shots were handy weapons for pirates to frighten their targets with